LISTENING AT PRAYER

also by Benedict Groeschel
published by Paulist Press

LEARNING THE ART OF PRAYER
(CASSETTE PROGRAM)

Learning to Pray in the Life of the Spirit
The Road to Recollection and Inner Peace
The Divine Readings—Prayer with Scripture
The Divine Liturgy—Prayer with Christ
Contemplative Meditation—The Inner Music
The Prayer of Life—Praying Always
The Contemplative Way—Preparing for God's Gift

ADVENTURES ON THE SPIRITUAL JOURNEY
(CASSETTE PROGRAM)

The Longest Journey: The Spiritual Journey Within
The Call of God—Beginning Every Day
Growing Integration and Purity of Heart
Overcoming Obstacles to Spiritual Growth—in Mind
    and Heart
Darkness and Its Uses for Self and Others
The Illumination—The Work and Prayer of
    Enlightenment
The Goal—Union and Peace While Waiting for God

GOD AND US (CASSETTE PROGRAM)

Our Creation and Being
Our Fall into Darkness—The Incarnate God
The Passion and Resurrection
Our Healing and Hope—The Holy Spirit
Our Mother—The Church
Our Eternal Destiny—Life After Death

Benedict J. Groeschel, O.F.M., Cap.

LISTENING
AT PRAYER

paulist press 🕊 *new york/ramsey*

NIHIL OBSTAT:
Daniel V. Flynn, J.C.D.
Censor Librorum

IMPRIMATUR:
†Joseph T. O'Keefe, D.D.
Vicar-General, Archdiocese of New York

September 1, 1983

Library of Congress Catalog Card Number: 83-61999

ISBN: 0-8091-2582-X (paper)   ISBN: 0-8091-0351-6 (cloth)

Published by Paulist Press
545 Island Road, Ramsey, N.J. 07446

Printed and bound in the
United States of America

CONTENTS

1 LISTENING AT PRAYER 1

2 WHAT IT MEANS TO LISTEN ... 6

3 LISTENING TO LIFE 16

4 LISTENING AT PRAYER WITH THE WRITTEN WORD 25

5 LISTENING AT THE LITURGY .. 60

6 PREPARING FOR CONTEMPLATION 81

Dedication

On behalf of my Capuchin Confreres
this book is dedicated to the memory
of the Servant of God,
Father Solanus Casey, O.F.M., Cap.,
the greatest Man of Prayer
I have ever known

Acknowledgement

The writer of a book on prayer must be indebted to an immense number of people who have taught prayer by word, example and writing. My first teachers were my parents and I am everlastingly grateful to them and all who came after. Father Zosima in *The Brothers Karamazov* calls prayer a great arc that reaches from earth to heaven and back again. One is deeply grateful to be part of that arc of life, desire and love.

Specifically, I am very grateful to those who have helped with the preparation of this book. Special thanks go to Sister Miriam Francis Perlewitz, M.M., Ph.D., of the Maryknoll School of Theology, who offered her professional advice on the use of Sacred Scripture. I am similarly grateful to Father Thomas O'Hagan, S.L.L., of St. Joseph's Seminary, Dunwoodie, New York, and to Father Pasquale Papalia of Mt. Carmel Church, Montclair, New Jersey, for their suggestions on liturgical prayer. The preparation of the manuscript was generously done with the invaluable help of Charles Pendergast and the typing by Karin Samuel and Elaine Barone. I am grateful to them and to John Lynch and Ted Weiland for proofreading. This book owes its existence to the suggestion of Dr. John Farina of Paulist Press.

1 LISTENING AT PRAYER

If you are one of the increasing number of people who seek to grow in the life of prayer, and if you would like to become more Christian in your response to God and your neighbor by means of personal prayer, then this book may be written for you. Admittedly, many excellent books on prayer already exist to explain its practice and theology and to suggest helpful techniques. So great is their number, in fact, that I was strongly inclined not to write another, even though several friends encouraged me to do so. As I prayed about it, I thought it might be helpful to write a simple book on a way of prayer I have found useful in my own life which abounds with distractions. It is a way I learned from many spiritual writers I have read since I started to pray as a boy. It has sustained me in my spiritual journey, which seems to have been a long struggle to survive, rather than any kind of a victory. In fact, I had to resist the temptation to call this book *Prayer for the Distracted* or *Mysticism for the Muddled*.

The way of prayer which this book suggests is so simple that it cannot be called a method; yet it is so powerful that I believe one can find it running through the lives of many saints and in many spiritual writings. *It is simply to listen at prayer.* If you learn to listen, then you will come not only to hear all creation praying within you, but you will also, faintly at first, hear Christ praying within you. St. Augustine tells us that we pray not only to Him, but with Him. He is the one who prays within us. If you listen you will be able to hear now and then the Holy Spirit responding to the Father and Son within you. Is it not too much to hope for—too sublime, too frightening? I don't think so, since the reality of God's presence within and all around us is the very foundation of all existence. Why should we not listen? One of the results of both psychological and spiritual growth is to become more aware of reality and to deal with it effectively. Accurate listening is an essential part of growth. In counseling we call this listening empathy, if done by a counselor, or insight, if done by oneself. We cannot deal freely with reality unless we first listen to it. The great living Reality is God's presence, above all things and in all things. The prayer of listening is a simple but direct road to perceiving that Reality.

Listening accurately is simple, but not easy. That is why even genuinely religious people often build their spiritual lives by doing things and saying things to God. It is easier that way. But as we all know even such genuine religion can become terribly complex. The prayer of listening makes things simple but it also makes us vulnerable, and that is frightening. Listening makes us open to Christ, the Word of God, spoken in all things: in the material world, the Scriptures, the Church and sacraments and, sometimes most threateningly, in our fellow human beings. To listen at prayer is to take the chance of hearing the voice of Christ in the poor, the weak, those whom we love and those whom we do not love.

Responding

It is a well-known axiom of the psychology of perception that we succeed in listening only if we respond in some way to what we hear. Like all perception, listening is a two-way street. If I do not respond, at least within myself, I don't really hear. But often we are not inclined to respond to God's voice within us. In that case, no matter what ideas or images fill our minds, we do not pray in reality.

This is a book about listening to God and responding to Him. It is about listening to Christ and praying with Him; it is about listening to the Holy Spirit and working with that Spirit in all the events of life. To grow in the ability to listen is a slow process. At first we hear and respond infrequently. Then we do it a bit more, and then, over the years, even more. This gradual growth in listening can cause us now and then "to hear the morning stars sing with joy" (Jb 38:7). It can plunge us into frightful conflicts! "If today you hear His voice, harden not your heart" (Ps 95:7-8). We must

3

often listen for "a gentle breeze in the midst of a whirlwind" (1 Kings 19:13). But if we continue to learn the prayer of listening, we will hear His call "Follow me." Listening, we are told, will even be our mode of prayer after this life. If we listen faithfully we believe that we shall come to hear "a sound like the sound of many waters, like the sound of many harpers playing on their harps" (Rev 14:2).

A few weeks after I wrote most of this chapter, I was struck by the number of times I failed to listen to God speaking to me in daily events. I was challenged by events that seemed trivial, or provoked by my own self-will or that of others. How could God speak through the mean, the ugly, the trivial? Not that He is responsible for these things—quite the contrary—but His goodness can speak through them and call us to repentance and to a decision for the true good. I reproached myself for making it all sound too easy in my little book on prayer.

Then, one evening, I was struck by a fierce blinding pain in the small of my back that left me almost unable to breathe. As two frightened confreres raced me toward the hospital I was enveloped in a pain I had never imagined—a pain that blotted out memory, identity, awareness of time, and left only the core of reason and a partial ability to project the future. (Some readers have experienced this; those who have not should know it is a unique perception.) Questions come to mind in a flash: Is God speaking in the pain? Yes, I know He is. He let it show me the intense fire of the desire to live and the awesome possibility of death. I thought I was about to die since I could not breathe. Out of the past came a prayer, deep and unbidden like a thunder clap: "Lamb of God, who take away the sins of the world, have mercy on me." God spoke against the pain and fear. I am grateful that I had been taught to listen.

Perhaps you already know how to listen but do you listen when you pray? Do you listen when you live? Could you listen better? Do you feel guilty when all your prayer is listening and not doing? Do you listen when you remember the past or plan the future? Do you listen even when you stop dead in your tracks and realize that you have sinned? "But God called to the man: Where are you?" (Gen 3:9).

Do you listen when you are pleased because you have done good? Do you listen when you laugh and when you cry? This little book contains a few ways to listen when you live and when you pray.

2 WHAT IT MEANS TO LISTEN

Everyone knows that prayer is a lifting up of the heart and mind to God. But this description can leave us feeling a little empty since when we pray our resolution often wanes quickly and our heart and mind come crashing down to earth with a dull thud. Thus prayer can appear to be a futile exercise, like continuously throwing a ball into the air. Yet there are times when prayer is easy, when our mind and heart remain uplifted for a time and we feel that finally we are making some progress. Then, the next time: thud. One day we hear of a method of recollection, and, when followed prayerfully, it does indeed enhance our powers to meditate. Our minds and sometimes our hearts are lifted up for a longer time and come down more softly.

Learning one of these techniques has often changed a person's life. The problem with any method, however, is that it cannot be used at all times. There is work to be done, constant intrusion, and the need to relax at times; thus, the technique itself may become a burden. Then begins another chapter in a long list of futile attempts to pray. Perhaps we can learn something from all the techniques of recollection and the more traditional methods of meditation. They all have a common denominator: they help us to *focus our attention* on our inner life, or on some passage of Scripture, or some religious truth. They are ways of perceiving and responding to events within our psyche, our inner world of thoughts, emotions and intuitions. The question beyond all these methods is how to listen in all the events of life, how to begin to lead a life of prayer.

Listening and Not Listening

Let us start with listening in its most obvious sense: it is the perception of sound with our ears. There are many sounds around us that we do not perceive because we do not respond to them. We ignore them: the ticking of a clock, the distant sounds of wind in the trees, a bell ringing. But when we listen, there registers in our mind, "ticking, wind, a clang," and we say to ourselves: "a clock, a breeze, a bell." Then, and only then, have we *listened*. We really don't hear most of the sounds around us; in fact, if we live in a noisy place, it is a blessing we don't. What is true of the hearing of external sound is also true of our mind. Our mental world of thought, feeling and intuition is bombarded with inner "sounds" which we don't attend to because we don't respond to them. We have learned to be selectively deaf within ourselves. We realize this when we are with a spiritually mature person. We hardly notice a patch of blue sky, but the person of prayer sees for an instant the dome of heaven. We hear a disturbed person muttering to himself on a busy street corner, and if we notice at all we say, "He should be hospitalized." The person of prayer hears the muttering voice and more, because within he hears the "cry of the poor," and in that he hears the voice of the Son of God. The prayerful person responds with some gesture of kindness, some help, or, if nothing else can be done, with a prayer bringing the sufferer before God. The stream of prayer has flowed on within, effectively linking the outer and inner world.

Another example may illustrate how we often fail to listen, even when we try expressly to pray. We intend to pray, so we get ourselves to the liturgy. We have heard the words so often that our attention drifts off. We wish this person would stop coughing; the singing is awful; the priest is too hurried. A person of prayer is next to us. A glance tells us that this person is attending not only to what is happening at the liturgy in church, but to something else—to the Divine Liturgy celebrated in the Kingdom of God. We are surrounded by distractions, and this person is surrounded by saints and angels. Who, we might ask, is in touch with reality? Who is really listening? It is important to note that in both of these examples the person of prayer has not blocked out the information of the senses: the sick person coughing is perceived and yet the liturgy is attended to. But through the sensible perception the person of prayer has been able to attend to more, to the spiritual reality that goes beyond what is perceived by the senses. This is the valid meaning of the idea of transcendent reality, that reality which is in some way perceived beyond the senses.

There are many examples of this ability to hear and perceive more by listening within. The poet, the artist, the scientist, the philosopher, the theologian, often listen to realities that are beyond immediate sense-experience. A person of prayer, however, perceives the highest reality. Christ warns His disciples against being those who hear but really do not understand.

Steps to Listening

Before we do anything else, we must become convinced of our selective deafness to a great deal we should be listening to. We should also realize that we are tuned in to a good deal we should be missing, to a lot of scatter sound or noise. The realization that we are missing a great deal of reality is the beginning of an effective desire to pray. This conviction should be operative within us long before we kneel down or adopt a recollected frame of mind.

There are two different ways to listen effectively to the events of life: one is very active and precise, and the other is more intuitive and contemplative. The researchers tell us that one way is reflected in our psychological mechanism by *beta* rhythms and the other by *alpha* rhythms. It is not necessary to go into what this means in detail, but if you are interested the subject is well summarized by Fr. William Johnston in his valuable book on the psychology of meditation, *Silent Music*.[1] It is important if you wish to learn to listen that you recognize when you are functioning with the beta mode and with the alpha mode. Beta rhythms describe our mental functioning in our usual daily activity—working, cooking, driving—and in most recreational activities like playing ball, gardening, or watching TV (sometimes this last activity is done at a sub-human level of reception without response). Beta thinking tends to follow logical patterns of cause and effect and is usually directed to some explicit goal. If you live in a bustling city you probably know that you have to slow down your beta responses a bit when you go into the country. Alpha activity is generally more relaxed and is always more receptive. It takes in a whole experience without dissecting into parts and without pursuing some specific result. The most common alpha experience is enjoying music, unless one is a musician and paying attention to the technique, in which case beta rhythms are being produced. Many activities can be done in either the alpha or beta mode, but they will be more fully human reactions when they are done at least partly in the alpha mode. These include praying, enjoying the company of loved ones, walking in the woods or

---

1. *Silent Music*, New York: Harper & Row, 1974.

looking at a beautiful view or object. Good and bad things can be done in either mode, but they will be more intense if done with some alpha perception. What is more beautiful than the thoughtful and loving encounter with friends? And what is more sinister than the image in the Psalms of the man who meditates upon evil in his bed? Both can be alpha experiences.

It is obvious that to listen at prayer, to link the outer world of sense with the inner world of thought and feeling, it is important to be able to pray in the alpha mode. Leading prayer of others, for instance at a church service, may require a good deal of beta activity. But this prayer will be a shallow experience if the leader is not somewhat recollected. I was impressed by the obviously recollected attitude of Pope John Paul II at his installation. Between being attentive to the needs of the hundreds of thousands who were present and the billion who watched on television, he was evidently truly recollected and able to link this distracting external event with his inner world of faith.

If you are not familiar with the two modes of thought reflected by alpha and beta rhythms, it is important to pause here and do a little personal introspection. Select an obvious practical activity—clean off your desk or make a phone call to arrange something. Then after a brief interval put on some soft music you like. Sit down, relax, close your eyes and take in the beauty of the sound. After an interval do the same with a prayer. First offer the Lord some prayer you know by heart and include a petition for yourself or someone you care about. Then relax and ponder what you have just done. You, a finite being, have spoken to the living and infinite God. Call to mind one of the two great symbols in the material world of the infinity of God—the sea and the sky. Now dwell without words on what you have just done.

If you succeed in these exercises, you have moved twice from beta to alpha thinking; you have listened within. You may be surprised at yourself, like the little boy who learned that all his life he had been speaking prose. You have often done alpha thinking, but randomly and not on purpose. Learn how to relax and do it, and you will have made the first step toward listening when you pray.

Listening with Mind and Heart

The ability to be recollected easily will not make us persons of prayer. In fact, recollection could be dangerous for some people: a form of escape or withdrawal from life. To listen prayerfully within it is necessary to engage the highest functions of both mind and heart: to know and to love. To pray with mind and heart is a most valuable human experience. A number of developmental psychologists have pointed out in recent years that interiority and recollection are integral parts of maturity and growth.

Our inner world is fed by what we receive through the senses, and this nourishment is integrated in recollection and prayer. To illustrate, let's assume we are at a liturgical celebration in which the Church brings to our senses a wide variety of experiences to focus our attention on the mystery of the Incarnation. Despite the noise of the Christmas rush (much of it left over from ancient pagan winter holidays), we hear the great message of the liturgical season and we reinforce it with our own personal reading. The advent verses and hymns, the readings from Isaiah and other prophets, and some personal reading on the Incarnation feed our mind with many thoughts on this stupendous mystery of the Christian faith. Then we pause. We enter into ourselves and allow our minds to try to grasp in one great sweep this reality of faith. But we come to an end, to a mystery which neither we nor anyone else can totally understand. The child is God and man, divine and human in one person. Heaven and earth are joined together...

Perhaps we choose a verse from Scripture, or a snatch of a hymn, "Come, let us adore," to keep this sense of mystery alive in us during the day.

We rise from our prayerful recollection and proceed about our duties, made a bit more hectic by the holiday rush. We are swiftly moving along now in beta. The streets are crowded. Then something we see or hear brings us back to our recollection. A phonograph record is playing in a store: "Come, let us adore." We stop and listen; we listen within ourselves. Then in the bustle of the crowd, totally unperceived by others, we adore. A little later as we are leaving the store, an old woman slowly hobbles along ahead of us blocking the way. We look. She is obviously lonely, a touch threadbare, a bit confused and frightened by the crowd. We take an extra ten seconds to hold the door for her and to smile. Her face brightens. We respond to her thanks with, "Have a nice Christmas." A sadness touches her face. She says: "Same to you." A feeling of pity knocks at the door of our heart. Although she has already disappeared in the crowd, we pause for a second: "God, help her, bless her, take away her loneliness...Come, let us adore." And so we have listened and so we have prayed. It may not seem like much of an event, but life is really made up of small events, of seconds. We will never learn to live the years prayerfully unless we learn by prayer to live the seconds deeply and well.

The experience described above is a simple one of listening and praying with mind and heart. It is important to recognize that the experience did not depend on the decision to do some act but rather on the decision to listen, to be attentive and to respond. We would probably become exhausted and frustrated if we started out with the resolution, "I am going to pray in the department store today because it is Advent." Such prayer would be a *tour de force* and would soon fizzle out. We only need to make the much more simple decision to listen and to respond with mind and heart. Life and its experiences will do the rest.

The example given above is a simple and appealing one. This is the way to learn to listen at the beginning. But we are going to move on to more challenging experiences—to listen to love and to hate, to joy and to sorrow, to peace and to rage. We must respond prayerfully to injustice, to sin, to death, to all the things that a thinking Christian must deal with creatively in life. The stakes are high because as Christians we believe we must deal with all the currents of life prayerfully and in the inner world of mind and heart. The Master has counseled His disciples to pray so as not to faint along the way.

3 LISTENING TO LIFE

The vital element of all spiritual growth is grace in its many forms: inner or sanctifying grace, actual grace or the call of God in the events of life, and finally the gifts of the Holy Spirit which make it possible for us to go beyond ourselves and our own strength.

Grace is a comprehensive term often used, as here, to include all the gifts of God to His children. These gifts are always given that He may ultimately give Himself to us. We may conclude, therefore, that the essential step of the spiritual life is to respond to the gifts of grace.

As we have seen in the opening chapter, to pray maturely is to listen and respond. Unfortunately, listening and responding can become a very nebulous procedure. There are people who think they are listening to God when, as St. John of the Cross points out, they are only listening to themselves. Are there practical rules or suggestions to help us avoid this danger? Can we sharpen and refine our prayers to insure that we are indeed listening to the voice of God in life and growing gradually in our ability to respond to it? The following simple suggestions flow logically from what we discussed in the first chapter.

I. *Listen to what life is saying in the present moment before trying to shape your prayer.*

The word "life" is meant here to encompass the complexity of events that converge on our conscious mind. From outside and from within, these events form a river of awareness, a stream of consciousness, which has been our constant experience of life since birth and possibly during the months before it. This powerful stream of awareness can be shaped and molded into human understanding only insofar as we accept it. Otherwise we move into an unreal world of our own making. This world is simply the projection of our fears and desires. It can only contain a god of our own making, a reflection of our own frightened ego. The false god of the unreal world may bear a resemblance to the living God. It may look like the Trinity or the Son of God, but it is ultimately a fraud. For the believer and especially for the Christian, the process of growth is a gradual repudiation of the unreal image of "god" and an openness to the true and living God. This is the spiritual process observable in the writings of the Hebrew prophets and in the work of spiritual formation which Christ undertook with His disciples. They resisted the message of the reality of the Messiah. They asked Him impatiently when He would triumphantly reveal His power to Israel. They looked for an earthly, unreal Messiah and found a heavenly, real one, but only after they had lost all their illusions and were forced by events to realize that His Kingdom is not of this world.

How do we listen to the reality of life and pray within it? The first step is to divest ourselves, as far as possible, of preconceived expectations of life. We have all been impressed by the rather simple souls who take life as it comes. They have an abiding awareness that there are many things in life which we do not and cannot control. They are often the most spiritual people we know because they listen to life and pray. Our unrealistic expectations of life are grist for the mills of neurosis. They cause us to worry, and then our prayer becomes a futile attempt to control God. We are so busy deciding what advice to give God about how to govern the world, and are so set in our needs and expectations of life, that we are unable to listen to any of life's real messages. Consequently, our prayer becomes an expression, albeit an intriguing one, of our own illusions.

II. *When life gives you its message, make the understanding of that message your first object of prayer.*

The virtue of hope is the foundation of the prayer of life. Hope is the grace to believe that whatever events occur, they will contain the necessary ingredients of our salvation. Hope does not pretend that all that happens is God's will. Many evil, untoward and stupid things

18

happen which are in no ordinary sense of the word God's will. Concentration camps cannot be called God's will. The crucifixion of Jesus Christ was not God's will, although He permitted evil to have its hour of apparent triumph. He did not summon legions of angels to deliver Him as Christ tells us He could have done. Rather it was God's will that His Son accept His suffering and with trust fulfill His perfect act of obedience in accepting the consequences of humanity. Since that day an endless procession of believers have done the same; out of the conflicts and often tragic circumstances of life, they have found the ingredients of their discipleship and growth in holiness. The prayer of life requires that we ask and wait for the grace to listen to what life teaches us.

Paradoxically, it is often the spiritually interested person with his own notion of God's will who is least prepared to listen. He will rage, fight back, suffer in silence, feel betrayed by God and man but will refuse to listen to what life is saying to him. He believes he already knows the message, so he has no need to listen.

The following event provided me with a moving example of a person who had almost no intellectual understanding of prayer, but who listened and then prayed. I once visited a leper colony in the company of a missionary who had told me of a remarkable old man living there. In this small colony of about two hundred Japanese people there were three churches, Anglican, Baptist and Roman Catholic. The missionary told me that many lepers in Japan were baptized Christians because their illness had drawn them to look for a deeper meaning to life. When we came to the man's tiny cottage, I discovered that leprosy had destroyed not only his hands but also his eyes and most of his face. Yet he was a happy, peaceful man. He told us he was grateful to have contracted the disease because when he was well he had led a wild, dissipated life; now he was seeking God and was filled with peace. No one looking on this frightful illness and hearing the tone of his simple statement could doubt that the man's words reflected his true state of mind. I was deeply moved as he touched his little statue of the Madonna and Child with the stump of his arm and told us of his devotion to the Mother of Christ. He was indeed a happy man. He had been able to pray with life because he had listened to it first. Life's powerful river of events, in his case painful events, had provided much of the impetus for a vibrant spiritual life. We have been told that it is better to enter life maimed or lame...

III. *Once the message of life has been received, you must try to integrate it with your attempt to live by the Gospel.*

We cannot pray in the way suggested unless we make the Gospel the focal point of life. Obviously, few of us live the Gospel values with any degree of perfection or consistency. If we wait until we are perfect to begin to pray, we will never get started. Insofar as we use our intelligence and will to live by the Gospel values, we will prayerfully integrate the events of life into our spiritual journey. Thus the events of life, like an unrefined natural resource, are made part of our ongoing life of grace. Actually, our success at prayerful integration is limited by our degree of commitment to the values of the Gospel. There is a dynamic link between prayer and living; as one improves in quality so does the other. This fact can be very disconcerting. We may fulfill the requirements of Church law, spend much time and energy doing good things and earnestly wish to follow Christ, and still discover that many of our values and desires are quite pagan and unconverted. The prayer of listening will help us confront precisely those areas needing conversion if we do not allow discouragement and worldly values to take over.

Because of the difference between our Christian hopes and aspirations and our worldly values, true prayer must often be conflicted. If we listen we can hear the clash between the "thoughts of God and the thoughts of men," but we struggle on. Prayer becomes truly Christian when we resolve to take the next good step in the right direction, i.e., on the Gospel path. We may be humiliated because it is such a small step and far from any enthusiastic realization of the teachings of Christ. It may be a faltering step which we suspect will lead to another fall or defeat. Or it may be a step from one un-Christian way to another that is a little less in conflict with the Gospel—a very sad and bitter experience. Francis Thompson called this "plowing the rock." We may simply pray for help for our unbelief and lack of trust. But if this is all we can do—and it is little enough—at least this prayer does not feed the illusion that we are anything more than unprofitable servants.

Thank God, often the attempt to integrate our lives with the Gospel is a more positive experience than the one described. Suddenly we see things in a new light. We discover a hidden truth which had always been there. We joyfully take a step in the right direction and our hearts burn within us. Our prayer is filled with light and joy, and we rise from it a bit further on the path of Christ.

Another experience, different from either trial or joy, is the prayer that becomes a solemn warning and a call to change. As we go about our business of life, we focus most of our attention and desire on accomplishing something vaguely related to the Kingdom of God, but much more related to our ease and self-enhancement. We have learned to be attentive to life, but then an event may happen to make us pause and, if we listen closely enough, hear something like the summoning voice of angels of which the Scriptures speak so often.

An example may prove helpful, since such experiences come to all of us now and then and can be the subject of prayer for months and years. Once while I was walking with a confrere in a very poor area of Atlanta, a dilapidated car pulled up carrying three young black girls, who were both curious and friendly. "Excuse me," the driver said, "but are you monks?" We replied that we were "friars." She smiled and said, "Oh, that is sort of the same family." After a little pleasant conversation, she asked me another question that will echo in my mind for years: "Are you out preaching the Gospel?" I wonder! I hope! I often doubt it. I fear that it may not be so—that this may be my judgment. I cry out for mercy and forgiveness. I try.

If I ever see her again, I must tell her that her question will echo in my prayer until the day I die.

IV. *Pray that you may pray.*

In summary we may say that the river of life's events provides a most powerful impetus for prayer. In the din of life He speaks to us, calls to us and providentially provides the materials of our salvation. We cannot tap this great stream in which grace unfolds unless we receive God's help. St. Augustine taught long ago that Christ was not only the way, but also the impulse for us to walk along the way. It is a valuable tool in the life of the spirit to pause and ask for the grace of prayer.

Human beings in all their religions have paused to pray in the morning and evening, to begin and end the day of conscious awareness with a prayer. The person interested in a life of prayer should take advantage of these two natural periods of rest to ask the help of the

Lord to sanctify the day by listening to His voice.

We need help to surrender our preconceived notions and fantasies, to go beyond our defenses and shallow expectations, to be lifted on the eagle wings of grace. To the one who seeks, it will be given; to the one who knocks, it shall be opened; to the one who listens, it shall be revealed.

4 LISTENING AT PRAYER WITH THE WRITTEN WORD

The simple step of listening to the summons to prayer in everyday experience must now be expanded to hearing God's voice as it comes to us in written words. Memorized verses, scrolls, and books have been a part of religion since human beings began recording words. No religion is without its book. The Bible, which contains the summary of Judaeo-Christian revelation, derives its name from the Greek, meaning "books." As we expand our prayer of listening, it seems logical to listen to the words of those who have written God's revealed Word, as well as to the writings of the saints and mystics who have heard the voice of God within. We will first consider listening by means of the printed word, and then go on to techniques for praying with Sacred Scripture and other spiritual books. Learning to listen at prayer with books is a big step toward integrating prayer into our lives.

Listening to a Book

We often hear printed matter read in a way that indicates that the reader has not made the words part of himself. A TV news commentator may read the words on a teleprompter over the camera. He is reading well and with a bit of feeling, but we know that these are not his own words. He passes, as he must, from reporting a fire, in which several children were killed, to a description of an annual boat race. In a sense, he cannot be part of what he reads. He cannot listen in depth; otherwise he would say, "Oh, hang the boat race and let's discuss our feelings about that fire."

The same is often true of readers in church who pass without much vocal distinction from the lamentations of Jeremiah to the warnings contained in the parable of the sower, to the announcement of a parish picnic. If the readers listened in any great depth, they might entirely forget the picnic, which they should not do since it is also part of life. The lack of a strong response to the public reading of Sacred Scripture may cause us to have a similar minimal response when we read it in private.

We often approach serious reading with the same mental attitude with which we scan the morning newspaper. A person may read countless prayers from Sacred Scripture and hundreds of books containing profound spiritual wisdom; yet he or she may have rarely listened to what has been read. What steps can we take to use our limited time more effectively in reading and listening to God as He speaks to us with written words?

To read with understanding, to listen to God's word, requires a conscious decision to be attentive so that we break the mind-set of superficial reading. This act is sometimes attempted by calling upon God's assistance, often in a most perfunctory way. To really listen, we must step back from the distractions of life, listen to the silence which shocks us for an instant, and pray with energy and attention for God's assistance.

This forceful and internal shift of our attention, called in psychology "changing the mind-set," is an important part of learning to listen, which we have already referred to in the general process of listening. Now we apply it to reading. We must say to ourselves, "If I am going to read this, I will read it well. If I am going to read the words of God, I will not scan them as I would a news magazine."

A prayer reminding us of our need for the help of the Holy Spirit has a twofold effect. It helps us change our mind-set and it reminds us that without grace we do not have the energy or even the inclination to listen to God. The intellectual conviction that we need help to listen must be backed up by desire. Desire goes beyond the immediate act of will which says "listen." It enlivens the will with the expectation of a pleasure or delight. We have all experienced desire or the expectation of delight when turning our attention to some reading outside a religious context. Remember how you felt when turning the pages of a riveting novel or reading a favorite magazine. Sacred reading will begin to fill us with a desire when we have learned to delight in it. Otherwise, it is a dull chore, performed with some bit of merit, but failing entirely to correspond to the words of

Christ, "I have come to bring fire to the earth, and how I wish it were blazing already" (Lk 12:49).

St. Francis was not much of a reader, but when he read, it was with attention to and delight in the words of God. He was even in the habit of picking up little scraps of sacred books that might have fallen loose. This should teach us a lesson. If we listen to Scripture with attention, desire, and delight, then even the pages and printed words will become sacred, i.e., precious and valuable. According to tradition, St. Francis summed up this idea in a prayer which was said for years by Capuchin seminarians:

Lord, I am Your most poor servant,
and unworthy of all Your good.
But I ask You to open to me Your treasures
    of knowledge
in such a way that I may love You,
for I only wish to know You that I may
    love You.

Another helpful mental step is to scan the passage to be read. It only takes a minute to look over a chapter of Scripture or the heading of a psalm, but it can mean the difference between simply reading words and listening to them. Reading well is an art even when the subject matter is not of a religious nature. A person should not read blindly, unaware of what is coming next, like a mole burrowing in the earth. He or she should survey the land ahead and consciously answer the internal questions: What am I about to read? What will it say to me?

Scanning is even more important in the case of religious reading that is already familiar. We have read the psalms and Gospels many times, but we must fit them into our present situation. The Liturgy of the Hours is a case in point. Its daily recitation can easily become routine and lead to inattention. For example, when I read Morning Prayer, I ought to look it over while considering my feelings: What do I think the day has in store for me? What is troubling me? What gives me joy? The prayer and readings may be consistent with my mood and situation, or they may be a counterpoint to them. (We shall discuss the possibility of a "counterpoint reaction" later on.) I must take the time to ask myself, "What will I hear from the Lord in this reading to help me with the day ahead?" I do not pray to change my mood or situation; I pray to learn how to deal with the day effectively as a struggling disciple of Christ. Let us look now at different kinds of reading, beginning with Scripture.

The Reading of the Psalms and Poetic Scripture

Most Christians are familiar with the endeavor to read biblical psalms and songs well. The serious believer lives with the psalms as part of life, often a part that has become repetitive and a bit burdensome. Whether by the priest or religious at the Liturgy of the Hours or by the folk singers at a high school liturgy, the psalms are repeated so often that we may fail to listen to them.

As we do with any Scripture reading, we must go through the simple steps of attention and desire described previously; in addition, we should begin with a special act of reverence acknowledging a revealed part of our faith: they are the words of God.

This realization doesn't make them easy to read. Most of us don't think in poetic form and so such words as "Awake, awake, lyre and harp, I shall wake the dawn" (Ps 57) do not always make it easier to listen to God. Because we are dealing with poetry—actually sacred songs—we must make a special effort to listen while we pray. This problem has been recognized for thousands of years. One way of treating it is a simple method called "the Senses of Scripture" which can be learned very easily.

A little attention at first may teach us this simple technique which we can use for the rest of our lives. Perhaps you will do best with this technique if you read it over now and try it as you go along. After you have finished this book, review this chapter for a greater understanding of the method. Learning it will take less than an hour. Keep a copy of the Liturgy of the Hours, a psalm book, or a Bible near you as you read on.

The Four Spiritual Senses of Scripture

Sacred Scripture can be read from many points of view. The following senses all represent devotional approaches to Scripture, and none of them are meant to replace the serious scholarly study of the Bible which seeks the accurate, original meaning of the words. According to your own reading level, you will find it helpful to review the scientific study of the psalms in order to learn some of the historical context and original meaning of this great spiritual literature. Such background information will enrich your understanding of each psalm and hymn and improve your ability to listen while you pray.

Apart from the original historical meaning, which is the object of continuing scholarly research, there are several other meanings or senses which were identified by the Fathers and Doctors of the Church as aids for praying the psalms. We will review the four most useful meanings and try to illustrate them so that, like the gears of an automobile, they may become familiar and be ready for use.

The Simple Literal Meaning

Usually we try to read a psalm as if it directly applied to us and are quite frustrated when it doesn't. For instance, the following quotations from Psalm 118 rarely, if ever, apply literally to any of us directly:

The nations all encompassed me;
in the Lord's name I crushed them.
They encompassed me about;
with the Lord's name I crushed them.

31

This text must be used in another sense (the allegorical), as we shall see. But how easy it is to pray the words of Psalm 139 and make them our own:

> O Lord, you search me and you know me,
> you know my resting and my rising;
> you discern my purpose from afar.
> You mark where I walk or lie down,
> all my ways lie open to you.[1]

Such a direct prayer can be made our own simply by following the preparation for listening at prayer which we have discussed. If we have time, we may ponder the psalm and reflect on such words as "my purpose" and "my ways." The psalm is a useful personal examination of conscience in the sight of the Lord.

The Allegorical Sense

This sense is probably the most important for listening at prayer with the psalms. The word allegory comes from the Greek, meaning "the other," and is a common literary device to indicate that the principal subject is described by another, or symbolic, subject. The reader is left the creative task of applying what is said of one to the other. This opens the mind to imagination and even more to intuition.

A beautiful allegory is found in Psalm 80,

1. These translations are taken from *The Liturgy of the Hours*, English translation prepared by the International Commission on English in the Liturgy. New York: Catholic Book Publishing Co., 1975.

where the psalmist speaks of Israel as a vineyard.

You brought a vine out of Egypt;
to plant it you drove out the nations.
Before it you cleared the ground;
it took root and spread through the land....
Then why have you broken down its walls?
It is plucked by all who pass by.
It is ravished by the boar of the forest,
devoured by the beasts of the field.

It is very clear from the rest of the psalm that allegorically the vineyard is the people of God. Here the meaning of the allegory is indicated by the text itself.

The allegory, however, has many other poetic uses, and often it is applied to a subject which is neither stated nor implied. For instance, it is not uncommon for ecclesiastical writers to apply a text like the following from Psalm 30 to Christ, even though it may not literally refer to Him.

To you, O Lord, I cried;
to my God I made appeal.
What profit would my death be,
my going into the grave?
Can dust give you praise
or proclaim your truth?
The Lord listened and had pity.
The Lord came to my help.

In general, such a text can certainly be applied to Christ, although scholars may debate whether it is a prophecy of the Passion. It can be applied as a broad allegory to many people, such as the martyrs, to whom death is neither the end of existence nor the end of their effectiveness in the history of the world. For example, this psalm could certainly be worked into a poem or play about St. Thomas More or St. Maximilian Kolbe. Using the text in this way would be an example of the broadest type of allegory, namely, applying the psalmist's words to someone he never had in mind when writing. How many times have we seen the words "Go to Joseph" on a shrine dedicated to the foster-father of Our Lord? Yet few perhaps realize that they come from the Book of Genesis and refer to the patriarch; they have nothing to do with St. Joseph literally.

The liturgy abounds with allegories of all kinds and it is not the purpose of the one who listens at prayer to speculate about their degree of literal accuracy. It is to our advantage to let the psalm or sacred song open our mind to rich images, new thoughts and shades of meaning, and opportunities to place ourselves imaginatively in the biblical situation.

With this in mind, may I suggest that you take up Psalm 22, which is in the Liturgy of the Hours for daytime prayer of Friday, Week 3. Spend some time letting the deeply moving description of the suffering Servant bring before you the familiar scenes of the Passion and death of Christ. The fact that our Savior recited the opening words of the psalm on the Cross adds to it a powerful message. If you are very attentive, you may hear Him saying the psalm within you.

Psalm 22 is an excellent introduction to reading many of the psalms as allegories of Christ. This kind of prayer with allegory is a simple and useful form of meditation.

The Tropological or Conversion Sense

The Greek word "to turn" gives us the next sense of Scripture, one that is very beneficial because it provides an opportunity for daily conversion or turning to God and away from evil influences. Because of the effects of both original and actual sin, and because of the deep, self-centered surgings of that mysterious sea called "the unconscious mind," it is necessary for everyone seeking genuine progress on the spiritual road to turn back daily to the light of God. Like a navigator at sea, we must check our bearings to see where we have drifted off course, or perhaps followed the false chartings of sinful traits. Among major world religions none omits the salutary exercise called "examination of conscience."

The Need for Daily Repentance

Unfortunately, in the immediate past, daily examination of life became a rather sterile counting of sins and faults rather than an opportunity for conversion. Many sincere Christians today are unaware of a need for conversion until they find themselves deeply enmeshed in sin; only then do they desperately call out to Christ for forgiveness. This situation could be avoided and a great deal of good done to others if we were to encourage more intelligently both interior and exterior penitence. Pope John Paul II, in a letter to bishops and priests, urged them to repent daily with these words:

> In consequence, we must all be converted anew every day. We know that this is a fundamental exigency of the Gospel, addressed to everyone, and all the more do we have to consider it as addressed to us. If we have the duty of helping others to be converted we have to do the same continuously in our own lives. Being converted means returning to the very grace of our vocation; it means meditating upon the infinite goodness and love of Christ, who has addressed each of us and, calling us by name, has said: "Follow Me." Being converted means continually "giving an account" before the Lord of our hearts about our service, our zeal and our fidelity, for we are "Christ's servants, stewards entrusted with the mysteries of God." Being converted also means "giving an account" of our negligences and sins, of our timidity, of our lack of faith and hope, of our thinking only "in a human way" and not "in a divine way."... Being converted means "to pray continually and never lose heart." *In a certain way prayer is the first and last condition for conversion,* spiritual progress and holiness.[2]

2. Pope John Paul II, Letter to All the Bishops and Priests of the Church, Holy Thursday, 1979. Boston: St Paul Editions, p. 28.

The Scriptural Prayer of Repentance

The Scriptures offer at least two aids to the prayer of repentance. One is the clear call to repentance, directed to the reader especially in the words of Christ, and contained also in the writings of the prophets and in the Epistles. The other call is more subtle and is found in the tropological sense of the psalms. We have all felt astonished and perhaps bewildered by the psalmist's curses of God's enemies or of personal foes. Many psalms describe a great conflict between God's followers and the pagans who eventually are routed because of His sovereign power. Often the psalm includes a reminder that the people of God were in trouble in the first place because they had been unfaithful. A look at the literal meaning of these "imprecatory psalms" will demonstrate that symbolically the great battle rages within ourselves: Israel represents my God-given strength and desires, while the idolatrous and murderous pagans are a symbol of my sins, vices and deep-rooted egotism. As I read the psalms allegorically, I recognize that I have often surrendered to or eagerly embraced these vicious tendencies within my mind and heart. In short, I have been an enemy of God. It is a relief to know that in the imprecatory psalms, at least, the friends of God are delivered by divine power (our virtues are victorious), while His enemies (the dark aspects of the human mind opposed to God) are defeated.

The following passages from Psalm 37 invite us to pray with this meaning because the enemies are not identified with a military force but rather with a sinister personal antagonist. As you read, remember that you are both the enemy and the good person.

> The wicked man plots against the just
> and gnashes his teeth against him....
> The sword of the wicked is drawn,
> his bow is bent to slaughter the upright.
> Their sword shall pierce their own hearts
> and their bows shall be broken to pieces.

How often has any person struggling to grow spiritually experienced the power of inner impulses, temptations, perhaps even compulsions which seem so much more potent than one's own virtues and strength?

> The just man's few possessions
> are better than the wicked man's wealth;
> for the power of the wicked shall be broken
> and the Lord will support the just.
> The Lord guides the steps of a man
> and makes safe the path of one he loves.
> Though he stumble he shall never fall
> for the Lord holds him by the hand.

The psalms do not exonerate us from our compromises with evil but they remind us of God's mercy and forgiveness in the midst of our struggle. The following words from Psalm 81 can often be applied to ourselves:

> O that my people would heed me,
> that Israel would walk in my ways!

At once I would subdue their foes,
turn my hand against their enemies.

Perhaps the most important aspect of this kind of prayer is the turning back to God and the consolation that the psalms offer the penitent. Because we naively expect the spiritual life to be without falls, we often fail to take the best advantage of them. Falls, great and small, can and do offer the individual an opportunity to grow, provided he or she is sincerely repentant. The depth of repentance cannot always be measured by its success, since many falls are related to psychological problems which may take years to overcome. Rather its depth is assessed by the individual's sincerity in recognizing and rejecting evil and the obstacles to spiritual growth, and by loving gratitude to God which is reinforced by genuine works of penance. Psalm 32 gives us one of many examples of repentance:

Happy the man whose offense is forgiven,
whose sin is remitted.
O happy the man to whom the Lord
imputes no guilt,
in whose spirit is no guile....
So let every good man pray to you
in time of need....
Rejoice, rejoice in the Lord,
exult, you just!
O come, ring out your joy,
all you upright of heart.

The Anagogical Sense

Perhaps the most profound sense of the psalms is the anagogical; it adds an essential ingredient to our life of prayer and suggests an elevating or transcendent experience. For a brief time, we join the choirs of heaven to participate in the joy of the saints to which we are called; we rejoice as if we were already in our heavenly home.

It may be objected that this does not sound at all realistic. It is not the kind of prayer that the contemporary Christian, aware of social responsibilities, should engage in. While such objections are heard often enough, they are based on a narrow view of reality. What is more real than the world to come in which we have our hope, and which will last forever? True Christian prayer must sometimes present that reality; the anagogical psalms fulfill that need. These psalms of praise call us to feelings of joy, thanksgiving and exultation, which we seldom experience in the humdrum of life. They are often put to good use in the liturgy to celebrate the Easter season, a wedding, or an ordination. Their most important use is to give us the opportunity, either in community or alone, to listen to the voice of hope which flows from the grace within us. Imagine the power of Psalm 46 when it was recited in the clergy barracks of Dachau concentration camp late at night after the prisoners had been locked in that miserable torture chamber.

God is for us a refuge and strength,
a helper close at hand, in time of distress:

so we shall not fear though the earth should
    rock,
though the mountains fall into the depths
    of the sea....

The Lord of hosts is with us:
the God of Jacob is our stronghold.

The waters of a river give joy to God's
    city,
the holy place where the Most High dwells.
God is within, it cannot be shaken;
God will help it at the dawning of the day.
Nations are in tumult, kingdoms are
    shaken:
He lifts his voice, the earth shrinks away.
The Lord of hosts is with us:
the God of Jacob is our stronghold.

A far more important use of this sense is the prayer of a faithful person beset by misfortunes who is reminded of joys that time will not wear away. For this reason these psalms are often put to best use by the poor. I have been deeply stirred to hear these psalms sung by the poor in their humble parish churches, surrounded by decaying buildings and faced with hopeless situations.

Perhaps you have experienced this unique spiritual joy when praying with the poor. If not, may I suggest that you go to some parish where you may hear Psalm 47 sung in English or perhaps in Spanish.

All peoples, clap your hands,
cry to God with shouts of joy!
For the Lord, the most High, we must fear,

41

great King over all the earth....
Our inheritance, our glory, is from Him,
given to Jacob out of love.

Although emotion may play an important
part in such an experience of transcendence, it
is neither its essence nor its foundation. The
ability to listen to the anagogical sense is based
rather on a profound conviction of faith in the
transcendent meaning of life: What we do in this
world has a significance that echoes in eternity.

This meaning is not founded on our own
lives which are transitory, nor on our will
which is equally limited, but on the power of
God and the everlasting life given by Jesus
Christ. Therefore, it is wholly appropriate to
use an anagogical psalm in the Mass of Christian Burial, or at a memorial Mass for the dead.
While a funeral should offer an opportunity for
the expression of grief and of prayer for the
deceased loved one, it must also express the
hope that transcends all earthly sorrow.

Listening with the Gospels

The good news of Jesus Christ contained in
the Gospels has been the source of Christian
meditation throughout the centuries. Even the
later books of the New Testament are in part
a reflection of the good news, composed in some
cases before the written Gospels were circu-
lated. The events of Christ's life became the
source of Christian meditation as the first
Christian communities were established.

A particular form of prayer inviting us to
listen to these events can be identified in the

early Church with the paschal commemoration both in daily liturgy and the annual celebration of the mysteries of salvation. This interior prayer is not strictly liturgical because of its very personal and individual character, but it can be deeply liturgical in another sense: it invites wholehearted participation in the public worship of the Church, which is based on mind and heart. Rather than viewing meditation on the life of Christ as something apart from the liturgical prayer of the Church, it is much more consistent with tradition to see the two as complimenting one another. Often in the immediate past, before the reform of the liturgy, the two forms of prayer had become rather distinct from one another—and perhaps still are.

Going to the Place

Listening to the life of Christ has often taken the form of placing oneself in the event, a prayer called "composition of place." Although this prayer takes many forms from para-liturgical drama to making the Stations of the Cross, in all forms the individual combines some knowledge of the Gospel with imagination. We try to put ourselves into the Gospel situation and elicit some appropriate personal response. We must have a basic understanding of the Gospel events, lest we create myths and obscure the reality of Christ's message. An example of this kind of myth-making is found in innumerable Christmas stories—from the legend of the roses that grew in the snow to the littlest angel of TV fame. Like too much candy, these can be dangerous to your health. Comprehending the essence of the Gospel narrative, placing oneself in it, and reflecting on one's response or lack of it can be a powerful prayer. Such popular devotions as the Rosary and Stations of the Cross had precisely this purpose and still fulfill it when intelligently used.

One of the simplest ways to go about such a meditation is to do a bit of serious reading, say, at the beginning of a liturgical season. While reading should be informed, it need not be scholarly. It is best to read from several points of view: liturgical, scriptural, and theological. We may choose something from the Church Fathers that relates the mystery of the season to our own spiritual life. The Liturgy of the Hours also provides a rich source of meditative reading for the liturgical cycle. With this background the individual may follow the liturgy from event to event, from prophecy and parable to historical occurrence in a meditative reflection that goes on from day to day. Advent-Christmastide and Lent-Eastertide are, of course, the best times for this kind of prayer.

A productive method of meditation is to place yourself at the scriptural event and ask: What does it mean to me? How can I respond to it? If by personal insight you are drawn into the event, the prayer becomes all the more effective because the imaginary elements will symbolically represent particular needs which you have. They may be far away from the actual historical event, but they do link you with it. For example, you might speculate about your actions if Christ were born in your neighborhood. Would you stay home? Would you go over to "the other side of the tracks" to see Him? Would you believe in Him if He belonged to a minority group? He did, you know. All these questions can bring the mystery alive for you.

After placing ourselves in mind's eye at a particular Gospel event, we may go on to ponder the reactions of those present at the historical occurrence. This enables us to examine our real feelings, because we are projecting ourselves into the role of a participant or a bystander.

St. Francis did precisely this when he prayed at the Christmas crib in Greccio. He became one of the shepherds of Bethlehem. When he popularized the Stations of the Cross he became one of the few faithful disciples who went with Christ to Calvary. You can do the same, but your meditation will be more fruitful if you let negative as well as positive feelings surface. For instance, you may want to ask God why the terrible events of the Passion could not have been avoided. This question may reflect your own resentment toward God about some problem or suffering which has come into your life and which seems bitterly painful and meaningless.

I have often meditated on the incident of the man with the withered hand and tried to place myself in his situation. He comes into the public life of our Lord early on, in Mark 3:1-6. It is a dramatic moment and one of the earliest recorded conflicts between Christ and His critics. The man is cured on the sabbath; after witnessing the miracle, Christ's enemies leave the synagogue plotting to destroy Him.

The man who had been cured was quite ordinary, filled with ordinary thoughts. He no doubt had to contend with all the fears and frustrations of a disadvantaged person. In a simple agrarian society the embarrassment of his affliction was not mitigated by good manners; a handicap was often seen as a sign of God's displeasure. How did he feel when he was cured by Christ? He was delighted; his parents were vindicated. He showed his restored arm to everyone in the town, which was probably Capernaum. I thought of this man as I sat in the town's old marketplace, no doubt near the place where it had happened. I could hear him relating the good news, laughing, and clapping his two hands together.

But how did he react later when he heard the controversy about Jesus of Nazareth? At first he defended Christ loudly to all comers. But if he was an ordinary man, he started to pull in his horns when he heard about the displeasure of those in power: the scribes, the priests, the Romans. Controversy was not his line. Someone suggested that it was all just a natural phenomenon; others thought it was the work of the devil. My God, the devil! What had he gotten himself into? He took his older brother's advice, "Keep your mouth shut, and don't go showing your hand to people."

Then the word went around that Jesus had predicted the destruction of the town. He had told people to drink His blood. He had cured the sick but had condemned the authorities. Many people who had been disciples followed Him no longer. The poor man put his head in his hands and was deeply perplexed. "After all," he said to himself, "if He is a prophet, He can save Himself. He does not need my help." And then, he remembered, "they killed the prophets, too."

One afternoon the Roman dispatch-rider brought news. Despite the fact that it was the great sabbath (he heard the news outside the synagogue), word spread that the prophet was dead. He had been crucified. The thought crossed his mind: "My brother was right. Keep your mouth shut." Then another thought, "Will my hand wither now? I have to go home and keep a constant watch for any signs of withering. Will it start to rot like a leprous hand?"

He started to pray to the Almighty. But suppose the prophet had not come from God? He began to feel sick....

A day or two later—on the Monday after the Sabbath—the news broke. Again, the Romans had it first. They were alarmed. Soldiers were everywhere. In public, everyone kept quiet, but underneath, there was wild curiosity, laughter, and, in the homes of His followers, great rejoicing mixed with confusion and disbelief. The man looked carefully at his hand. It was perfectly all right. No signs of decay. He laughed; he cried. He clapped his hands together. Jesus was a prophet, after all, and had come back from the dead. That will fix them! They'll all believe now; they'll *have* to. He spoke to his brother and suggested: "Let's tell everybody." But his brother again said, "Keep your mouth shut. Wait." So he said nothing. He was still silent when the rebellion came. The Romans razed the town and crucified him with the others. Perhaps he called on the Prophet when they pierced his hands.

Listening to Christ, the Prophets, and the Apostles

As an altogether different experience of prayer, we should listen carefully to the teaching of Christ our Lord, as well as to those of the prophets and the Apostles, especially St. Paul. Throughout Scripture there are teachings addressed to particular audiences which, however, apply to all Christians in various ways. Listening to these words in such a way that the word of God echoes mightily in one's inner being is a form of prayer essential to the Christian spiritual life. Obviously the general form of the prayer of listening already outlined is especially adapted to the prayerful reading of Sacred Scripture. There are, however, several suggestions which will assist the reader to apply them during periods of prayerful reading. These suggestions may reveal whether you are reading Scripture carefully and fruitfully.

1. *Never read or listen to Scripture as if it were some other book. The words of God, Cardi-*

nal *Newman tells us, must never be treated like the words of men.*

To read Scripture is to hear the voice of God. Reverence, attention, and prayer should always be a part of such a reading; otherwise Scripture may become like great music which has been heard too often. We should begin by calling on the Holy Spirit to help us in the true reading. This kind of reading is to some degree beyond our natural processes because we must read with the gifts of faith and love.

2. *Read intelligently. Make use of commentaries, lessons and explanations of Scripture.*

This need not be done every time one reads. It is helpful, therefore, to read in some orderly fashion, after having consulted an appropriate commentary. Commentators should be chosen whose specific purpose is to help the reader grow spiritually. The world has never been lacking in writers who are so abstract and objective that they fail to communicate the message. There are those, too, whose goal it is to "debunk" the Bible.

3. *The words of Scripture must always be heard in the context of the Church, lest the individual become his own holy spirit and his own little church.*

We need not be scholars in order to listen prayerfully to the words of Scripture, especially the teachings of Christ and St. Paul. However, we should know the true meaning of the words and understand the situation in which they were originally spoken. Reading Scripture with strong feelings and emotional response, but without adequate intellectual preparation, poses the danger of hearing the message out of context. If the reader is not intelligently prepared to study a passage in its historically accurate context, he is likely to read from his own narrow point of view. This personalized context or idiosyncratic point of view is always present psychologically and can be the source of much prejudice and narrowness.

The Church wisely has always been against "private interpretation of Scripture" simply because it canonizes the individual's limited experience into a reflection of the divine reality. The Church has never maintained that the Holy Spirit does not speak to the individual, but it has, of necessity, adhered to the principle that individual interpretation and response must always be within the context of the whole Christian community and its tradition.

Although there are many advocates of "free personal interpretation," inevitably they have established some norms of agreement (a tradition) in which they read and pray. Whether fundamentalist or unitarian in outlook, they have had to agree on a context outside the individual reader's subjectivity in order to avoid religious anarchy. This frame of reference or context has usually been very narrow, reflecting the social values of a particular class, location and time.

The context of the Catholic Church is very wide. It begins with the early Christian community reflected in the later books of the New Testament and expands to a variety of ages, times and places, all of which are bound together by tradition and the pastoral teaching of the Church, which is historically concretized in the bishops.

To escape the dilemma of becoming another "holy spirit," it is important to read within this greater context. Usually this context is psychologically and sociologically provided by active membership in the Church. When the local church fails to provide an engaging and appealing informal context, many people, who are drawn by grace and valid religious experience, may reject the traditional context (or more often be unaware of its existence) and read the words of Scripture in light of their narrow world vision. When the Church is abused as an expression of personal ambition or as a vehicle for worldly power and wealth, the local church is brought to the edge of destruction. Such a situation prevailed on the eve of the Reformation. Many fervent Christians, failing to find a spiritually enlivened presentation of the traditional Christian context from the local bishops and church, moved in varying degrees toward personal and private interpretation.

In his fascinating book, *Agenda for Theology,* a Methodist theologian, Dr. Thomas Odin, has issued a call to the Protestant world to return to the broader context of Christian tradition.[3] He has suggested that Protestants, who take Scripture seriously as the Word of God, read the Church Fathers and Doctors and the teachings of the early Councils. Paradoxically, many Catholics are now reading very much in their own personal context and are all but unaware of the Catholic tradition. Others pay attention only to "scientific" approaches to Scripture which are often not primarily intended to nourish the spiritual life.

The fact that so many have taken to reading Sacred Scripture today marks a great leap forward in life. As someone who grew up with only the Douai translation, I am very grateful for this development. I memorized so much of the old English text that phrases like "sufficient for the day is the evil thereof" still echo in my mind. Anyone interested in religious literature today is likely to read Scripture. While much has been written on biblical subjects, it seems to me that there is still insufficient popular reading material relating scholarship to the tradition of the Church and especially to the many spiritual writings which make up the richest resource of Christian literature.

If you want to read Scripture for personal spiritual development, you may have to shop around to find something suited to your own reading level. Often the most helpful material

---

3. Thomas C. Odin, *Agenda for Theology*. San Francisco: Harper & Row, 1979.

is written not on Sacred Scripture but on the spiritual life by authors who attempt to incorporate tradition and contemporary scholarship.

4. *Along with the great themes presented during the liturgical seasons, individual themes for prayerful listening to Scripture may offer an effective way to pray.*

At times we need to look for and listen to a particular message in the teachings in Scripture. Our need may be related to our life experience. If someone dear to us is terminally ill during the Christmas season, we may wish to read the Passion accounts in the Gospels, even as we participate in the joyful liturgy. Often the two activities can be interestingly interwoven.

Perhaps our development will suggest a particular intellectual search. It is normal in the course of spiritual growth to be confronted by such questions as: "Why all this stuff about sin and repentance? Isn't it rather neurotic?" These questions should not be ignored. They may be shelved for a while until we have the leisure to look at them, but they should be faced. The best way to deal with them is to look up the relevant texts in Scripture and begin to listen to them prayerfully. Inevitably, the texts will be from one of the prophets, or from a New Testament writer citing the teachings of Christ.

Not long ago, I spoke with a religiously committed young man who had serious questions about Christ as Savior and Son of God. In the turmoil of adolescent moral confusion, he joined the charismatic renewal and found great help and meaning in a personal conversion to Christ. Although he had attended Catholic schools for twelve years during the 1960's and 1970's, he felt that his religious education was inadequate, at best. He began a systematic study of Scripture and took several courses on the New Testament.

One day he asked himself a question concerning Christ: Whose Son was He and how? The problem deeply upset him because each answer opened another question, which led to other issues: revelation, grace, the transcendent, and ultimately to God. The memory of his encounter with the Lord was real and painful. Was the encounter true or was it an illusion? I suppose he came to me because I work at being irrelevant. Being a child of the megalopolis, I share with most of my fellow New Yorkers a certain skepticism about trendy answers to the questions of eternity. We have seen the ultimate answer come and go so often that, if we believe in anything, it is usually something classic, something that has lasted for at least a thousand years.

I looked for something to help him in his difficulty: a classic work yet something modern, something traditionally Catholic and relevant to the needs of a young person. I gave him *Redemptor Hominis,* the first encyclical of Pope John Paul II on the place of Christ in the Church and the world, and I asked him to study it prayerfully. I suggested that he have his Bible at hand, along with a few decent commentaries, and, using the encyclical as a guide, start to pray his way to an answer. I strongly recommended a few important texts for study and prayerful, deliberate reading. Beginning with John 3:16 and continuing through Romans 5 and 8, the words of the Pope, interlaced with quotations from the Fathers and Vatican II, revealed to him for the first time a whole powerful Christology.

As often happens when a person does this carefully and prayerfully, the words took fire in his heart. The same grace of the Holy Spirit which had called him at the time of his initial conversion came to him anew. He was not just studying; he was praying and listening to God's Word. Every fiber of his being responded to the Word. Christ spoke to him not only as an historical person but as a living reality in the Eucharist. Christ had been calling this young man since birth and baptism; now he was listening and responding within the context of the Church.

My own reward was an interesting one. The young man wanted to share with me his enthusiasm, his fire, the response of his whole being. I was grateful and rejoiced with him. He seemed to forget, however, that I had long since worked my way through these texts. I now listened to other questions, words, texts, and teachings. He could not know I had confronted the questions of life and death in the flood-tide of youth. He could hardly be expected to realize the fire which an older person experiences when he reads John 21:17-19:

> Then He said to him a third time, "Simon, son of John, do you love Me?" Peter was upset that He asked him the third time, "Do you love Me?" and said, "Lord, You know everything; You know I love You." Jesus said to him, "Feed My sheep. I tell you most solemnly, when you were young you put on your own belt and walked where you liked; but when you grow old you will stretch out your hands, and somebody else will put a belt round you and take you where you would rather not go." In these words He indicated the kind of death by which Peter would give glory to God. After this He said, "Follow Me."

"Were Not Our Hearts Burning Within Us?

This exclamation (Lk 24:32) of the disciples who met the risen Christ on the road to Emmaus captures the experience of listening prayerfully to the Teacher in Scripture. This may not happen every time we read; if, however, it never, or only rarely, happens, something is wrong with our spiritual life. Even in time of darkness and trial the words of Scripture will take fire in our hearts. Excerpts from Scripture were often scratched on the walls of dungeons where martyrs had been tormented: "Have patience; I am coming soon." These people had learned to listen well in life so that they might listen at the time of death.

Praying with Spiritual Writers

Included in the literature of the Church are writings of great Christians, some of them saints and others just struggling, fervent souls, who left us their personal prayers and meditations. Although almost all of these writings may have been inspired by grace, they do not share the special inspiration and authority of Scripture. The Church has taught that even the writings of canonized saints are valuable for their own intrinsic argument, but must not be looked on as another form of public revelation. In a word, you are free to agree or disagree with St. Francis, St. Teresa, St. Bernard and others.

Though they seldom admit it, the disciples of many saints often disagree with their patrons on one thing or another. The question here is how to pray with a spiritual writer — whether it be the first-century Church Father St. Ignatius of Antioch, or the twentieth-century monk Thomas Merton—and the answer is: Gratefully but carefully. Gratefully, because it is a blessing and a joy to come across a writing or prayer that expresses our own needs and experiences. For this reason many Christians have their favorite authors, who may change during the process of their growth. Sometimes a person may stumble upon a spiritual writer who will serve as his or her guide for decades. This happened to me as a teenager when I picked my way through an impossible old English translation of the *Confessions* of St. Augustine. I shall be grateful to that great teacher for the rest of my life.

Whoever the writer and whatever the prayer, all must be accepted with a certain care lest we inject our own personal point of view into their writings and prayers. As we have indicated, misuse of Scripture can lead to inventing a false Christ. The same may happen when we read an intriguing spiritual writer. As a monk, Thomas Merton was troubled by the expectations of others which were unreal but which came from the reading of his books. Spiritual authors tend to put their best efforts into print. The rest is burned up or thrown away. Keep in mind that a writer is giving you his or her best; give your best to incorporate that message into your life, rather than idolizing the author.

If your favorite spiritual author is deceased, find out at what stage in life he or she wrote the books or meditations. Do they reflect the writer's thinking as a young or inexperienced person, or as someone in trouble? If a writer is still alive, remember that the chosen guide may have a change of mind.

Having said all this, I should add that we can learn many lessons, some almost too profound for words, by absorbing the writings, prayers, poems or meditations of great spiritual authors. Sometimes they can be tucked away for years and then come to the surface as a real grace. We should be listening for such messages.

I once had the privilege of offering Mass in the cave of St. Ignatius Loyola at Manresa in Spain. As I paused after Communion, the well-known Latin prayer attributed to St. Ignatius spontaneously unrolled like a scroll in my mind: *Anima Christi*... "Soul of Christ, be my sanctification..." I had forgotten that I even knew the prayer in Latin but every word came to me effortlessly. I have found ten years of use for that prayer, often repeating it several times a day. I am grateful that I listened.

5 LISTENING AT THE LITURGY

The title of this chapter, indicating that we should be receptive at the liturgy, may cause many readers to be uncomfortable. To those who grew up before the liturgical reforms following Vatican II, it may suggest a kind of passive piety and highly individualized devotion which, at least from this point in history, looks dreary. To a younger person the actual meaning of the suggestion, "listening at the liturgy," may be almost incomprehensible. Liturgy has become an act—something you do. When well done it should involve the active participation of everyone present. Along with these two points of view, others hold a variety of opinions ranging from those who with great relief would return to the personal silence of the old liturgical usage, to those who are put off by any ritual requirements at all and are uncomfortable with any symbols that speak to us of mystical or unseen reality. Finally, many Christians—who appear to be increasing in number—regard the liturgy as a sacred drama or spectacle. They are enthusiastic about listening, but I am using the word differently.

My first impulse when writing this chapter was to convert you all to my own point of view. But later I regretted my sin when I realized that that should not be my goal. I'm not a liturgist, and my purpose is not to enter the symbolic battlefield of liturgical combat. This is a book on ways to listen at prayer. Hopefully, whatever your liturgical bent, this chapter may assist you to listen at the liturgy.

Listening to the
Liturgy of the Word

Much of what was said in the last chapter applies directly to the first part of the Mass, the liturgy of the Word. The same attitudes of receptivity and response, of listening and answering, apply to the liturgy in a preeminent way. In the present form, the liturgy exhorts us with beautiful verses to respond to the readings in an enthusiastic way, not only with voice but with mind and heart. How rich an experience it can be to cast ourselves into an attitude of listening and responding, especially when we decide to set our minds in the true frame of reference of this event. This means that in the *now* moment of our lives we hear the words of God Himself, the deeds of His Son, and the call of the Holy Spirit in our lives. Christ is truly present and speaks in the sacred liturgy through lector and homilist. The gift of reverence or fear of the Lord is given to those who courteously listen.

Listening at the Holy Banquet

One can listen to the Word of God when reading alone or even more powerfully at the Offices of the Church, the Liturgy of the Hours. But there is a unique experience of listening and responding which can be found only in the celebration of the Eucharist itself. Without entering into theological controversy, let's consider what we may listen to and how we may respond in prayer.

The Community

The community of believers, the faithful of Christ, should always be represented at the liturgy. There may be only one other person, there may be a handful, there may be thousands in a stadium. But the community always speaks, even if it is with a priest and a single participant representing the community. And the community demands a response. We gather with body, mind and spirit, with virtues and vices, with the conflicts generated by grace and sin, and with hopes and fears. To fail to listen to the voice of humanity in celebrating the mystery of salvation is to miss the dimension of the Incarnation. From Genesis to Revelation, the message is one of God's coming to be with His children, of Christ among His brothers and sisters, of the Word made flesh and dwelling among us.

Admittedly, when we listen prayerfully to the community, we often hear discordant sounds and receive conflicting messages. It is hardly a choir of angels. So one must listen with a tolerance bordering on humility, and with a sense of reverence for how the Lord is working out the salvation of others, and with an openness to their needs. To be comfortable praying with a community no doubt requires a sense of humor. Humor will help us to pray with, rather than to be disturbed by, the old man who confesses his little sins out loud or the child who keeps asking questions about where God is.

People who try to pray at the liturgy open themselves up in a surprising way, even those most proper and reserved. If their presence is anything more than mere attendance, they are aware that they are publicly witnessing their inmost thoughts, their aspirations for God and their desire to know and serve Him. Prayerful involvement in the liturgy means proclaiming oneself a penitent, a child of God and disciple of Christ, and one who hopes for eternal life. Thoughtful and mature prayer at liturgy is far more than that. To be present where two or three are gathered in His Name is to be more open to humanity than perhaps at any other time. People need to express this in different ways; none should be superficial and none should be aloof.

The Paschal Mystery

The liturgy of the Mass is the celebration of the central mystery of redemption. It is in a way the only event we can participate in, whose reality is rooted in both eternity and time, in the domain of being that is beyond time, place and number, and yet in human history. The liturgy brings the Cenacle, Calvary, the Resurrection, and Pentecost to each of the worshipers. It brings us to the day of eternity, not simply by a consideration of that reality but by a mysterious participation in that once-for-all sacrifice of Christ.

Though celebrated hundreds of thousands of times daily in varying circumstances—with pomp in cathedrals and with stealth in concentration camps—there is ultimately only a single celebration which unites all, priests and faithful alike, in that everlasting sacrifice of salvation and praise which is the life of the saints. We begin our life of eternity, our heaven, by participating (such a weak word, but there is no other) in the praise of the Son. Without getting into the theological mechanics of a partial explanation of this reality (for it is a mystery and all explanations must be inadequate), we may identify two key elements in the eternal praise of the Triune God in heaven to which we are called and in which we participate.

One element is the worship of praise and thanksgiving, which we, who are created out of nothing, joyously offer to the infinite and personal Being who created us and called us to share His life, His eternity. If the world had not fallen, this description alone would sum up the life of the blessed and it would begin in worship and praise on earth. This praise is the common element of all authentic prayer and worship of all human beings on earth right now. It is the underlying reality that gives some unity to worshipers among all the great religious traditions.

The other element is the Paschal Mystery. Briefly, this mystery means that we are a people, fallen, wounded, lost, and then saved by sonship in Christ and promised eternal life; we are united with the Son of God as He offers to His Father the worship of a world redeemed. The worship, praise, and thanksgiving of the human family is thus transformed into a sacrifice of praise, accomplished by the Son on earth, Jesus of Nazareth, the Lamb of God who takes away the sins of the world.

One must be careful not to become overwhelmed by all the ramifications of the Paschal Mystery. One could spend a lifetime meditating on the different aspects of this mystery of praise as one could gaze with a telescope into the mystery of the evening sky. There is no end of wonders.

Our question here, however, is not how to understand the central mystery of our faith more intelligently, but rather how to participate in it more prayerfully. How can we listen to this mystical reality, and how can we make our own prayer at the liturgy a true personal participation in it?

Here we must again use the powerful gift of imagination. We have no way of intellectually conceiving what eye has not seen. For this reason the liturgy is surrounded by symbols. In dealing with symbols imagination is of great importance, as it is in the use of allegory which we have discussed in the psalms. The following technique is an attempt at receptive prayer by using imagination to help us to become personally involved in the totality of the Paschal Mystery. This should be done without neglecting the reality of the liturgical celebration we are attending at the moment. My structural guide in formulating this imaginative attempt is the Eucharistic Prayer which, like a pyramid, leads us from the Church on earth to the Church of the holy souls on their journey, to the worship of saints and angels, subsumed and united in the single sacrificial prayer of Christ.

We begin at the top of the pyramid with the great prayer called the Dialogue and Preface, where the whole Church on earth proclaims its debt to Christ, the Redeemer and Savior. Imaginatively we may see Him now in glory, surrounded by the mysterious angel hosts. He is the Second Person of the Trinity, without beginning or end, the Alpha and the Omega, but still He bears the marks of earthly life. He is of Eternity but not a pure spirit. He has a body more real than yours or mine because it cannot corrupt. He has a heart that beats, and unlike any corporeal process of life that we know, it shall never cease. His breath shall never come to an end, His thoughts shall never grow old. It is a body whose mysterious and endless functioning represents our own hope of personal immortality. But there is something apparently discordant about this Person who brings earth and heaven together. He is wounded. In His hands and feet are deep wounds, now glowing and shining with life, present now as they were at the Resurrection. Although He is the Son, united in the Triune Godhead, He is also one of us. To Him we pray as God; with Him we pray as man.

Pause for a moment to imagine this scene symbolically. The red-robed priest is in the shining light described in Revelation. His mother is at His side; she is a being of earth, formed as we are formed. Once a humble peasant woman who stood by the side of the gibbet of death, she is now all dazzling bright. She is queen but no aristocrat, a queen of mercy and love. She is the first of those redeemed by Christ. She is the first member of the Church, and therefore she stands at the head of the choir of innumerable saints making motherly intercession for us.

Although your imagination may fill your mind with a glory and brightness that is unparalleled, there is absolutely nothing aloof about these two figures. They are often depicted as regally distant, but this is simply not true. They reach out, beckon to you with the utmost intimacy. No human love of mother and child, of husband and wife, or of friends is an adequate image of the love which these two persons extend to us. It is individually directed to each of us, although the two mysteriously reach out to countless multitudes. Individuality in multiplicity, unity in diversity—these are abstract terms that have been used to describe the quality of beauty. This love and beauty are not abstract.

Mysteriously, the attention of the High

Priest is directed to each person, and yet it is also completely directed in loving communion to the Father and the Holy Spirit, in what can appear to us only as a well of indescribable light.

His wounded hands are raised in a Son's intercession and all creation offers thanks to Him. Our human words may somehow suggest the essence of this worship. We know these words so well—offering all creation through the God-Man: "This is My Body; this is My Blood."

The Intercession and Prayer for the Holy Spirit

If you have been drawn into the Paschal Mystery and have listened to the inexhaustible contents of the words of Eucharistic institution, you may be a bit startled that they are followed by petitions of a rather down-to-earth sort, for the shepherds of the Church, for the Christian community and in fact for the vast number of human beings who can be said to be seeking God. Personally, I have come to see these intercessions as a healthy jolt back to the time-bound and earthly situation in which we as members of the Body of Christ on earth participate in the Paschal Mystery. We can't stay in heaven no matter how enticing this prospect may be. Our vocation as Christians in the world binds us very much to the Church and to the whole human family.

Confronted with this reminder of our human condition, of the context of our lives in this real but passing world, we soon turn to the Holy Spirit. It is by His gifts that we are one in the unity of faith and worship, and, if we are willing to let His gifts operate in us, in the unity of charity and mutual concern for each other.

The Saints

We should pause for a moment to consider the choir of saints in adoration and loving union with the prayer of the High Priest. In the Eucharistic Prayers, the needs of the Church and of all the human race are linked to honoring and commemorating the saints. This is a beautiful joining of time and eternity, a reminder that the ultimate purpose of our lives on earth is to join in the everlasting destiny of the saints.

If your imagination is not yet overwhelmed, you might pause to consider some representation of the saints. Like Christ, they are, each to his or her own degree, totally absorbed in the worship of God and yet intimately united with each other. We have no image of such a union of relationships. The best image we can conjure up is one given by Sacred Scripture of an immense choir joyfully singing in harmony; each member is an individual yet each is part of a single river of joyous praise.

Like most of us, you probably feel that you know someone who joined this heavenly choir immediately or soon after death. Surely we must all know many people there. The Church has provided us with a list (a canon) of models who were heroic in their lives; it teaches that they are in that reality which Christ calls "My Father's house." Don't be afraid to join with these saints at Mass. Canonized or uncanonized saints are great friends and the best of models. At the liturgy we can join our two realities together—earth and heaven. Both words fall short of expressing what they mysteriously contain. Know that Christ and His saints make intercession for us during our earthly life—an existence that is trying, fascinating and conflicted but which has the promise of eternal life.

The Church in Purgation

Finally, as we come to the end of the Eucharistic Prayer, we are reminded of that other equally mysterious reality, the individuals *in via,* those who have not entered our Father's house but are on their way. Catholic tradition calls this experience "purgatory." We ought to take this experience seriously since with all our best endeavors we will probably be in it. Let's simply call these loved ones "those who have gone before us." We know something of the reality they experience. They are being purified for entry into the supreme reality of eternal life. They are completing earthly tasks done poorly or left undone. The saints tell us that these have one regret, one pain: they have yet to take their final place in the Kingdom. We sometimes hunger for God; they have this experience in its totality.

St. Catherine of Genoa, a mystic who had visions of their reality, described them in beautiful terms, saying that they see before them "our Beloved God, His arms wide open ever calling them by mighty looks of love."

In the Eucharistic Prayer the Church always remembers them and has prayed for them since the earliest times. In the liturgy our two realities meet and touch. It can be a most moving part of the day to be together in the reality of the Paschal Mystery with those who have gone before us, to help them and to be helped by them in the prayer of Christ.

The Prayer of Glory

The Eucharistic Prayer ends with a simple prayer of glory to the Trinity through our own High Priest. If you have been attentive, it is possible sometimes to catch some of the power of this simple prayer of glory, to experience the hymns of the saints, the longings of those on their way, and the desire of those on earth who seek God.

The Lord's Prayer

With the completion of the Eucharistic Prayer at the moment when the community joyfully chants its "Amen" to the great doxology, the faithful are now invited to continue their prayer to the Father, using the words of His Son. It is as if the heavenly choir pauses in its endless praise and those who have gone before us in their journey, and we, the noisy, conflicted, confused, sinning and repenting Church, we have our moment, our prayer. It has been given to us by the Lord when He walked the earth, and its content, unlike the prayers of glory, is only relevant to this life. There are no other words so simple and solemn that sum up our needs as well. Because of their simplicity we can put into them all that we are and experience. In the liturgy we offer a single childlike petition for all humankind: for present and future generations.

Travail and Peace

The prayer, "Deliver us, O Lord," called the embolism of the Lord's Prayer, reminds us that the Church on earth is always in travail. Finally, in the peace of Christ, we pray for each other, trying to lay aside our negative feelings and emotions before we receive the Lord in Holy Communion. This prayer for peace should never be said lightly. Symbols of peace which are not true or genuine inject a note of conflict or superficiality into what is most solemn.

The Cry of the Soul

We now come to the prayers that prepare us for the sacramental meeting with Christ. These prayers—the Lamb of God and the prayer before Communion—are powerful and deeply personal acts of humility and expressions of dependence on divine mercy. Since the day when I thought that death was near, they have taken on a new and heightened meaning; the *Agnus Dei* has come to express my only hope. At the breaking of the bread we may meditate on the mystery of Christ's broken Body being the source of unity, as we, the members of Christ, are joined and nourished as one.

If one takes the sacramental Communion with Christ seriously, it is especially important to live through these prayers and savor every emotion they stir up. I often wish that a longer pause were permitted at this point in the Mass so that we might prepare ourselves with greater recollection. In the words of the great Hymn of Preparation prior to the great entrance in the Byzantine Liturgy, we should "lay aside all earthly care as we prepare to welcome the King of All." If one ponders seriously what is about to take place in Holy Communion, the only sentiments that are mentally healthy and help us adjust to this reality are humility and confidence in God's mercy.

The Sacrament

For most prayerful Catholics listening at the liturgy means meeting Christ the Savior in an intimate, if mysterious, way. The act of adoration to the reserved Sacrament on entering the church, a devotion very much related to St. Francis of Assisi and his personal love of Christ, is the actual beginning of prayerful listening for most of us. Those who are uninformed concerning devotion to the Real Presence are deprived of a powerful psychological help in preparing themselves for prayerful listening. If one has prepared by signs of reverence on entering the church, and during the liturgy, then the genuflection of the priest before the reception of Holy Communion has much more significance. The adoration of the Sacramental Presence is a perfect preparation for the sacramental reception of the Eucharist which is an even more powerful personal experience of relationship with Christ. Communion then becomes a time of internal listening.

Properly, the reception of the Eucharistic meal should be the communal and personal climactic moment of the whole liturgical participation. This experience or participation is best considered as a whole, rather than as a series of events competing with one another for importance. At times a confused emphasis on the reception of the Eucharist has caused some people to regard the liturgy as a machine for producing consecrated Hosts. This is a most unfortunate distortion. One listens and responds to Christ prayerfully during the *entire* liturgy, even though for psychological reasons the reception of Holy Communion followed by the quiet awareness of union with Christ may seem to the person at prayer to be most moving. Certainly the time of recollection and thanksgiving after Communion should open us to listen to the Son of God as He acts in our lives. It should call forth prayerful sentiments, generosity, trust, repentance and love. It is not simply a time to listen—it is *the* time to listen.

Difficulties

People often ask: "How do I listen to Christ at these precious moments? How do I respond to this most holy and intimate part of my spiritual life?" Common, too, are these thoughts:

"Here I am in my difficult and unimportant life in the presence of the Word of God, the living Savior by whom all things are made. It is the most cherished moment of my day. Never at any moment, even with my loved ones, will I be more loved than I am right now in the presence of Love itself and I can't say anything. I cannot keep my mind from distractions, from meaningless or even unruly thoughts."

This is a familiar experience. In fact, it is my suspicion that the period of silence after Holy Communion is often unduly shortened or taken up with inappropriate singing because people are unconsciously trying to escape from the uncomfortable experience of failure to pray in an intimate way. Instead of being a beautiful communal expression of interior listening to Christ, the hymn becomes a denial of our failure. On the other hand, a solemn reverent hymn after an appropriate silence can be most powerful.

What can be done about this spiritually depressing failure to really pray during Communion? Perhaps the great mistake is to begin with the expectation that the sacramental meeting with Christ must involve the emotional trappings and sensations we experience when meeting some famous person. We expect some spontaneous emotional reaction. We feel we should be impressed, moved, or touched without any apparent effort on our part as we might be if we met a famous government official or well-known prelate. We are disappointed. There is no "roar of the crowd." We don't feel elation spontaneously.

We are also distressed in the presence of Christ by our own shortcomings and failures. None of us loves with a pure heart, nor have we overcome completely our darker side. Here we are in the presence, veiled though it be, of Infinite Purity and Love. Like Adam and Eve in the garden, personality hides in the leaves and trees of distraction. Christ waits quietly in the shadow of the inner temple of our being. He does not intrude. Faith, like a flickering sanctuary lamp, tells us He is there. But unless we focus on His silent presence which reflects the humility of God, we shall not really listen to Christ in His sacramental presence.

Speaking and Listening to Christ

Most devout people try earnestly to speak to Christ with some formalized prayer, often taken from the psalms. More adventurous souls speak to Christ in spontaneous words of love and gratitude, praise and petition. Both activities are a great step forward. Then, choral or instrumental music will serve as either a backdrop for prayer or as a final communal expression of adoration. An even better prayer at this time is "to listen" to Christ in the manner already discussed.

Those who seek to pray in this way must take into account the following: (1) shortness of time, (2) the psychological reactions of fear, guilt, or resentment which the proximity of the Son of God may unconsciously stir up, and (3) the anxiety of having to "make the most" of this time.

"Listening" under such circumstances

implies that we make a specific conscious resolution simply *to be with* Christ. Christ is with us throughout the day and night. He is before us, behind us, above us, and below us, as we are reminded in the beautiful ancient Irish hymn, "The Deer's Cry," often called "St. Patrick's Breastplate." When receiving Holy Communion we ought simply to accept, focus on, and—if I may use the phrase—let ourselves be submerged in the presence of Christ. Just *be!*

Soon enough, unless you are rather advanced in prayer, distracting thoughts will enter your mind and unwanted emotions will surface. Instead of trying to shake these off, I have found it beneficial to try to grasp one of these thoughts and look at it in the presence of Christ who seeks my sanctification more than I can ever imagine. Perhaps the distracting thought is a fear that has been troubling me. Silently I present it to my Savior, who overcame the fear of the Cross. I share my fear with Him in silence. Sometimes He answers me in a very subtle way. In my mind I can see a wounded hand, pierced with a nail. Sometimes I struggle with an unruly thought—an unresolved anger, a resentment or passion. In ways that human words are not able to express He reminds me that He once lived in this world, that He experienced these things Himself, or saw His friends and disciples struggle with them. The Christ who waits in the silence of the Eucharist is mysteriously a Christ of flesh and blood. Thus He is revealed; thus He is experienced. "This is My Body." This is such a profound moment in the liturgy that the Roman

Missal stresses the importance of a silent period of reflection at this time.

If you are one of those tarred with the brush of modern psychological skepticism (and I feel sorry if you have been so tainted), you will no doubt say, "All this sounds like auto-suggestion and a projection of my need to be close to someone." To be sure (except in the rare case of a genuine mystical apparition) we do not have the mental equipment to be directly in touch with a presence that exists outside the world of material things.

To be in touch with Christ's presence we must make use of what our intelligence and memory tell us (the truths of faith, and in this case the mystery of the Holy Eucharist), and of our own pattern of response to others. This means that to some indefinable degree the Christ we meet in interior prayer will bear the stamp of our own perceptions and personality. But the objective teachings of faith with a vibrant apprehension of the historical Christ, along with our participation in the worship of the Christian community, will converge to make our experience more authentic.

If All Grew Silent...

By allowing the real issues of the interior life—our emotions, needs, conflicts, joys, and sorrows—to surface in His presence we may be able to make our Savior's words operative in our own lives. Once we express these concerns to Him, they become silent within us. It stands to reason that the more silent we are, the more deeply we can be aware of our needs. At the same time, to the degree that we put anxiety to rest, the reality of Christ will speak to us in every dimension of our inner being.

The following quotation from St. Augustine has been my guide over the years in trying to cope with the reality of Communion. Although the event described did not take place at the liturgy, it has helped me to appreciate the meaning of the silence that may enfold us at this time.

> If to any man the tumult of the flesh grew silent, silent the images of earth and sea and air: and if the heavens grew silent, and the very soul grew silent to herself and by not thinking of self mounted beyond self: if all dreams and imagined visions grew silent, and every tongue and every sign and whatsoever is transient—for indeed if any man could hear them, he should hear them saying with one voice: We did not make ourselves, but He made us who abides forever: but if, having uttered this and so set us to listening to Him who made them, they all grew silent, and in their silence He alone spoke to us, not by them but by Himself: so that we should hear His word, not by any tongue of flesh or the voice of an angel nor the sound of thunder nor in the darkness of a parable, but that we should hear Himself whom in all these things we love, should hear Himself and not them: just as we two had but now reached forth and in a flash of the mind attained to touch the eternal Wisdom which abides over all:

and if this could continue, and all other visions so different be quite taken away, and this one should so ravish and absorb and wrap the beholder in inward joys that his life should eternally be such as that one moment of understanding for which we had been sighing—would not this be: *Enter Thou into the joy of Thy Lord?*[4]

The Final Prayers

The final prayers of the liturgy after the personal thanksgiving must appear a bit anticlimactic. What else is to be said? Indeed, this may explain the brevity of the conclusion of Mass.

Perhaps the best attitude is summed up in the dismissal and blessing. It should be a joyful—or at least hopeful—experience. The final prayers should prepare us for what is ahead, and the blessing should be a special reminder that the Lord is with us as we go about our duties, enjoying our blessings and facing our trials. These prayers and blessing are obviously very communal: following the communal and very personal experience of Communion, they recall that we are, above all, members of the Church—the community of God and the body of Christ.

---

4. St. Augustine, *Confessions,* trans. Frank Sheed. London: Sheed and Ward, 1978, IX, 10, pp. 158-159.

6 PREPARING FOR CONTEMPLATION

Contemplation, which has been described in many ways, is used here in its narrowest sense: the simple awareness of the presence of God which is a complete and generous gift beyond any effort or merit of the individual.

St. Bonaventure maintains that contemplation is the life of the blessed in heaven, insofar as it is possible to experience it during our earthly pilgrimage. Contemplation is often characterized as a certain seeing of the Divine Light; however, one can use the word "hearing" as well as "seeing," because the awareness goes beyond any sensory perception and, indeed, beyond all that the mind can comprehend. The drives, senses, desires, thoughts and complex ideas of reason are not divorced from contemplation, but stand like foothills around this highest peak of human experience—a peak to which no one can ascend unaided by grace and the gifts of the Holy Spirit. Our purpose here is not to teach a method of contemplation (in my opinion a contradiction in terms) or even a way to contemplate because I haven't found one yet, if indeed we may say that there is a way. St. John of the Cross maintains that the way is "no-way." Our intent, rather, is to apply the simple technique of listening to discern whether it can be a remote preparation for coming to God as He is, and not as He is reflected in created things.

We have followed the process of listening to God on the levels of revelation proceeding from His single Word, which is utterly simple and has neither beginning nor end. In a rising fountain of beauty and love we have listened to Him speak in the material world, in the events of daily life, in our relations with others, in His prophets and saints, and in the words of those who have sought Him sincerely. We have listened to Him in the words of Scripture and in the most sacred of all sounds to fall on human ears—the words of His Son recorded in the Gospels. By using imagination, Scripture and tradition, we have tried to capture some of the reality of the eternal liturgy, the Paschal Mystery, in conjunction with the living signs of that reality in the prayer of the Church.

We come now to the possibility of some experience, (I hesitate to call it a perception) of that God in whom we live and move and have our being, who is heard in all things and yet is beyond all things.

If, by listening, you hope to approach this experience, then you must take certain steps not in order to draw God to you but to open your inner eyes and ears to this possibility.

I. *Reaffirm your belief that contemplation of God is possible and desirable, and that, if you have not yet experienced it, you might come to this form of prayer.*

Many people set out on the road to contemplation but never make much progress because they take many detours, become involved in false issues, or try to build spiritual castles from their own ideas. They can adduce "good reasons" for not becoming a contemplative, but their thinking indicates an erroneous concept of this reality. "A contemplative approach will separate me from others; it's unreal religion; it's not incarnational."

This distorted view of contemplation is frequently a rationalization for not wanting to pay the price. True contemplation is intimately related to the rest of life. If one cannot prepare for this gift on a street corner, then one cannot prepare for it anywhere. While such things as external silence and order certainly help the process of listening and the task of coming to grips with oneself, they are no more necessary for contemplation than a loudspeaker is necessary for God. He has spoken and will continue to speak in all circumstances to those who will listen.

II. *In preparation for this gift you must strive to place no limitations on God's word, nor act on preconceived notions or personal preferences, so as to clear the way for His action in you.*

This is the task of a lifetime, to be approached with wisdom and patience. Indeed, except for the greatest saints, we all desire God and many other things besides. We really do want and need acceptance, love, a peaceful life, our daily bread. We desire these things for ourselves and for those dear to us. This is not wrong, but if our ability to trust God (and be led by Him) were stronger than the anxiety produced by these desires, this anxiety would be relinquished and we would be free. But we cling to our anxieties and erect obstacles to the possibility of contemplation. The capacity to receive the grace of contemplative prayer is proportionate to the individual's ability to be willing to surrender all things less than God. We should not play the martyr or try to fool ourselves with a veneer of trust which makes us appear in our own eyes to be quite beyond where we actually are. In the midst of fears and worries, we should stop and ask, "What is God saying to me in this event?" The more we choose, with His help, to accept the reality that is here, the more we prepare for the perfect gift of Himself.

We should not be impatient for this greatest of gifts. Since contemplation is the highest experience possible to human beings, it is beyond all good deeds and all good gifts. Contemplation is what the eye has not seen, nor the ear heard, nor has it entered into our hearts to imagine. A contemplative life is not to be achieved in a day, a year, or a decade. The way is slow and painstaking, and we would make no progress at all unless God in His mercy guided us.

The desire for success and achievement, which haunts us from childhood, is a persistent obstacle to contemplation. This desire has made many sincere souls settle for less—for some amalgam of virtue and vice, some experience of grace mistakenly called contemplation. Many settle for prayer experiences which are like magic lantern-views of heaven, or those saccharine paintings of the heavenly court that decorate old churches. Such experiences may be helpful along the way, but they are not contemplation. We suffer from dryness and aridity when such "consolations" disappear. We should rather be glad to lose them. Contemplation is not like that. It is like "the sun shining from the east to the west." It is the coming of the Lord.

III. *You must be prepared to grasp and to treasure the sparks or flashes of contemplative experience, the distant muffled sounds of God's presence, when they come into your life. Walk while you have the light.*

It seems to me that the invitation to brief periods of contemplation comes often to the person struggling along the way. It is not that God is far away: rather, the center of our attention is far from Him. Nevertheless, like a traveler nearing the coast we hear the distant sounds of the sea or catch a whiff of the salt air.

It is important to make a mind-set to stop and listen, to take in, however briefly, the faint traces of God's actual presence in life. This mind-set is one of quiet, of darkness, or unknowing. As we have pointed out, it will only complicate matters if one pretends that one has had this experience. "Be still and know" is the best advice. One can trust this awareness of God all the more if it manifestly does not come from our own needs, if indeed it contradicts what we are thinking and goes against our inclinations. If our attempts to grasp the voice of God always reaffirm our desires, then we may be projecting our needs and recreating our familiar false gods.

The contemplative experience of God, however faint, should leave us changed, wounded perhaps, like Jacob after his struggle with the angel, but a bit closer to that transformation which is our life in Christ.

Christian contemplation, because of the doctrine of the Cross, may embrace experiences which are sorrowful as well as joyous. The Carmelite nun, Edith Stein, wrote that she had the most beautiful gifts of prayer as she awaited death in Auschwitz. The light of contemplation is so bright that it can shine into the darkest human experience. St. Stephen's cry during his stoning that he saw "the heavens thrown open and the Son of Man standing at the right hand of God" (Acts 7:55-56) is a very early affirmation of the power of the contemplative gift to defy all circumstances of trial and confusion.

The Contemplative Life

Perhaps this is the moment to discuss the notion of a "contemplative life." Sometimes this term is used to describe a "cloistered life," that is, one set apart from the world. Although it is a reasonable expectation that those called to a cloistered life will be growing toward contemplative prayer, they are not the same thing. A distinction is sometimes made between an "active" life and a "contemplative" life. I have always found this distinction wanting in many ways although it is used even by great authors. It seems to me that this distinction is perhaps best made in terms of the psychology of individual differences. Some people seem from childhood to be drawn by a greater sense of interiority and a need for order and others by a tendency toward action and work. A "contemplative lifestyle" may appeal to the former and apostolic action to the latter, but contemplation is not dependent on one or the other. Contemplation is God's gift to those who follow Him with generosity and a pure heart. It can come to persons of either inclination, and in either case will be obstructed by self-will.

Even human weakness does not block the coming of the Lord to those who seek Him with purity of intention. Scripture and Church history are filled with examples of people like Mary Magdalene, Charles Péguy and Francis Thompson, who struggled with great internal wounds and yet came to some contemplative knowledge of God. A truly contemplative life is one in which the individual listens to God the Father, to Christ and to the Holy Spirit. Like the life of the greatest contemplative, Mary of Nazareth, it may be lived in the humblest circumstances and amid the most disturbing events. To begin to live a contemplative life, you must honestly attend to the brief experiences of contemplative prayer described above and allow them to shape your vision of life and your desire. God's providence will lead the way and give you what you need. You have only to be willing to listen to His Word.